First hundred words in Spanish

Heather Amery

Illustrated by Stephen Cartwright

Translation and pronunciation guide by Jane Straker

Designed by Mike Olley and Jan McCafferty

 There is a little yellow duck to find in every picture.

En la sala

In the living room

 **el papá**
Daddy

 **la mamá**
Mommy

 **el niño**
boy

2

la niña
girl

el bebé
baby

el perro
dog

el gato
cat

3

Vestirse   Getting dressed

los zapatos
shoes

los calzones
underwear

el suéter
sweater

4

la camiseta
undershirt

el pantalón
pants

la camiseta
t-shirt

los calcetines
socks

5

En la cocina
In the kitchen

el pan
bread

la leche
milk

los huevos
eggs

la manzana

apple

la naranja

orange

el plátano

banana

Lavar los platos
Cleaning up

la mesa
table

la silla
chair

el plato
plate

el cuchillo

knife

el tenedor

fork

la cuchara

spoon

la taza

cup

La hora del juego — Play time

el caballo
horse

la oveja
sheep

la vaca
cow

la gallina

hen

el cerdo

pig

el tren

train

los cubos

blocks

De visita
Going on a visit

la abuela
Grandma

el abuelo
Grandpa

las zapatillas
slippers

12

el abrigo
coat

el vestido
dress

el gorro
hat

En el parque
In the park

el árbol
tree

la flor
flower

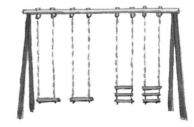
los columpios
swings

el balón
ball

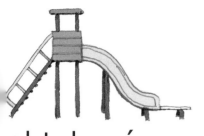
el tobogán
slide

las botas
boots

el pájaro
bird

el barco
boat

Por la calle   In the street

el coche
car

la bicicleta
bicycle

el avión
airplane

la camioneta
truck

el autobús
bus

la casa
house

Celebrar una fiesta Having a party

el globo
balloon

el pastel
cake

el reloj
clock

el helado
ice cream

el pez
fish

las galletas
cookies

los caramelos
candy

19

Nadar Swimming

el brazo
arm

la mano
hand

la pierna
leg

los pies
feet

los dedos
de los pies
toes

la cabeza
head

el trasero
bottom

21

En el vestuario
In the changing room

la boca
mouth

los ojos
eyes

las orejas
ears

la nariz
nose

el pelo
hair

el peine
comb

el cepillo
brush

23

Ir de compras   Going shopping

rojo
red

azul
blue

verde
green

amarillo
yellow

rosa
pink

blanco
white

negro
black

En el cuarto de baño   In the bathroom

el jabón
soap

la toalla
towel

el retrete
toilet

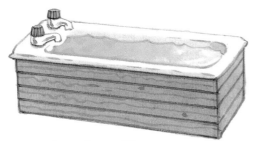

la bañera
bathtub

la barriguita
tummy

el pato
duck

27

En el dormitorio
In the bedroom

la cama
bed

la lámpara
light

la ventana
window

28

la puerta
door

el libro
book

la muñeca
doll

el osito
teddy bear

Match the words to the pictures

el balón

las botas

los calcetines

la camiseta

el cerdo

el coche

el cuchillo

el gato

el gorro

el helado

el huevo

la lámpara

la leche

el libro

la manzana

la mesa

la muñeca

la naranja

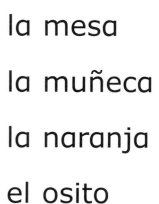

el osito

el pastel

el pato

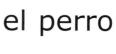
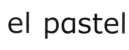

el perro

el pez

el plátano

el reloj

el suéter

el tenedor

el tren

la vaca

la ventana

Contar Counting

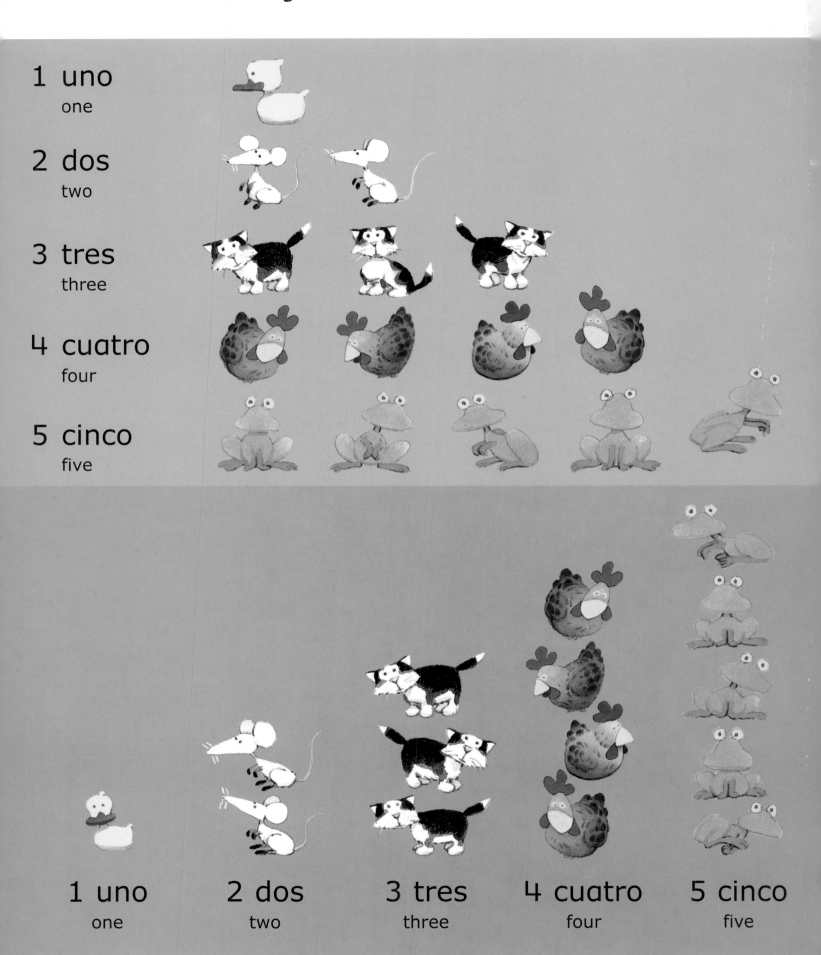

1 uno
one

2 dos
two

3 tres
three

4 cuatro
four

5 cinco
five

1 uno
one

2 dos
two

3 tres
three

4 cuatro
four

5 cinco
five

Word list

In this alphabetical list of all the words in the pictures, the Spanish word comes first, next is the guide to saying the word, and then there is the English translation. The guide may look strange or funny, but just try to read the words as if they were English. It will help you to say the words in Spanish correctly if you remember these rules:

Capital, or BIG, letters show which part of the word to stress:

a	is said like *a* in *hat*	
e	is said like *e* in *hen*	
o	is said like *o* in *horse*	
ch	is quite different from any sound in the English language, but it is said like the *ch* in the Scottish word *loch*	
rrr	is *r* rolled on your tongue, like the *r* in the name of the Scottish poet *Burns*	
th	is said like the *th* in *month*	

abrigo	*aBREEgo*	coat
abuela	*aBWEla*	Grandma
abuelo	*aBWElo*	Grandpa
amarillo	*amaREELyo*	yellow
árbol	*ARbol*	tree
autobús	*aootoBOOSS*	bus
avión	*abeeONN*	airplane
azul	*aSSOOL*	blue
balón	*baLONN*	ball
bañera	*baNYEra*	bathtub
barco	*BARko*	boat
barriguita	*barrreeGEEta*	tummy
bebé	*beBE*	baby
bicicleta	*beesseeKLEta*	bicycle
blanco	*BLANko*	white
boca	*BOka*	mouth
botas	*BOtass*	boots
brazo	*BRAsso*	arm
caballo	*kaBALyo*	horse
cabeza	*kaBEssa*	head
calcetines	*kalsseTEEness*	socks
calle	*KALye*	street
calzones	*kalSSOness*	underwear
cama	*KAma*	bed
camioneta	*kameeoNEta*	truck
camiseta	*kameeSSEta*	undershirt, t-shirt
caramelos	*karaMEloss*	candy
casa	*KAssa*	house

celebrar	*sseleBRAR*	celebrate
cepillo	*ssePEELyo*	brush
cerdo	*SSERdo*	pig
cinco	*SSEENko*	five
coche	*KOTshe*	car
cocina	*koSSEEna*	kitchen
columpios	*koLOOMpyoss*	swings
compras	*KOMprass*	shopping
contar	*konTAR*	counting
cuarto de baño	*kwartodeBANyo*	bathroom
cuatro	*KWAtro*	four
cubos	*KOOboss*	blocks
cuchara	*kootSHAra*	spoon
cuchillo	*kootSHEELyo*	knife
dedos de los pies	*dedoss-delossPYESS*	toes
dormitorio	*dormeeTORyo*	bedroom
dos	*doss*	two
fiesta	*FYESSta*	party
flor	*flor*	flower
galletas	*galYEtass*	cookies
gallina	*galYEEna*	hen
gato	*GAto*	cat
globo	*GLObo*	balloon
gorro	*GOrrro*	hat
helado	*eLAdo*	ice cream
hora	*Ora*	time

Spanish	Pronunciation	English
huevos	*WEboss*	eggs
jabón	*chaBONN*	soap
juego	*CHWEgo*	game
lámpara	*LAMpara*	light
lavar	*laBAR*	clean
leche	*LETshe*	milk
libro	*LEEbro*	book
mamá	*maMA*	Mommy
mano	*MAno*	hand
manzana	*manSSAna*	apple
mesa	*MEssa*	table
muñeca	*mooNYEka*	doll
nadar	*naDAR*	swimming
naranja	*naRANcha*	orange
nariz	*naREESS*	nose
negro	*NEgro*	black
niña	*NEENya*	girl
niño	*NEENyo*	boy
ojos	*ochos*	eyes
orejas	*oREchas*	ears
osito	*oSEEto*	teddy bear
oveja	*oBEcha*	sheep
pájaro	*PAcharo*	bird
pan	*pann*	bread
pantalón	*pantaLONN*	pants
papá	*paPA*	Daddy
parque	*PARke*	park
pastel	*passTEL*	cake
pato	*PAto*	duck
peine	*PEYne*	comb
pelo	*PElo*	hair
perro	*PErrro*	dog
pez	*pess*	fish
pierna	*PYERna*	leg
pies	*pyess*	feet
plátano	*PLAtano*	banana
plato	*PLAto*	plate
puerta	*PWERta*	door
reloj	*rrreLOCH*	clock
retrete	*rrreTREte*	toilet
rojo	*RRROcho*	red
rosa	*RRROssa*	pink
sala	*SSAla*	living room
silla	*SSEELya*	chair
suéter	*SSWEter*	sweater
taza	*TAssa*	cup
tenedor	*teneDOR*	fork
toalla	*toALya*	towel
tobogán	*toboGANN*	slide
trasero	*trassERo*	bottom
tren	*trenn*	train
tres	*tress*	three
uno	*OOno*	one
vaca	*BAka*	cow
ventana	*benTAna*	window
verde	*BERde*	green
vestido	*besTEEdo*	dress
vestirse	*besTEERse*	getting dressed
vestuario	*bestooAReeo*	changing room
visita	*beeSEEta*	visit
zapatillas	*ssapaTEELyas*	slippers
zapatos	*ssaPAtoss*	shoes

This edition first published in 2002 by Usborne Publishing Ltd, Usborne House, 83-85 Saffron Hill, London EC1N 8RT, England. www.usborne.com Copyright © 2002 Usborne Publishing Ltd. The name Usborne and the devices ⬨ ⬨ are Trade Marks of Usborne Publishing Ltd. All rights reserved. No part of this publication may be reproduced, stored in a retrieval system, or transmitted in any form or by any means, electronic, mechanical, photocopying, recording or otherwise without the prior permission of the publisher. First published in America 2002. AE. Printed in China